Heart *and* Soul

by

Elvis Stojko

with a
Review of Competitions
by
Penny Mallette

Edited by Gérard Châtaigneau

Rocketeer Publishing

Elvis Stojko with Ed Futerman

Original Text - *Elvis Stojko*

Concept and Design - *Gérard Châtaigneau*

Management /Legal - *Ed Futerman*

ISBN 0-9682314-0-3

Printed in Canada

C O N T E N T S

FOREWORD

Not only am I a fan of Elvis, but I am also a friend. To be asked to write this foreword is truly an honour.

I remember seeing Elvis at a small sectional championship when he was probably eight or nine years old. Even at that young age, he stood out from the others, not just for his jumping ability, but for his quick feet and enthusiasm for speed.

As a junior skater, Elvis moved to Orillia, Ontario, to train under my coach, Doug Leigh, and to skate alongside me. I was always amazed that a young person could be so curious about technique and so passionate for quality. Every day there were questions and discussions about skating, and on every session I had another set of eyes watching my every move. The great thing about Elvis was that he didn't want to mimic my skating or anyone else's. He wanted to be his own skater and his own person.

Already, Elvis has made his mark in skating, and he is one of the most important skaters of all time. Although he is a technical genius, he has turned technique into an art form. His keen sense of rhythm and timing give him an accuracy that no other skater possesses.

For me, achieving the status of World Champion was truly an emotional and proud moment. But, seeing Elvis - upon whose career I may have had a small impact - achieve this status, was equally gratifying.

Elvis will be successful in all his endeavours. He has strong work ethics and wants to be the best. For him the word "balance" does not end with skating. Family and friends are a priority, and he has discovered that the ability to create "harmony" is all important.

Brian Orser

Quest for excellence

"What's past is prologue."
Shakespeare, *The Tempest* (1611)

At the 1991 World Championship in Munich, Germany, Elvis Stojko completed a quadruple toe/double toe jump combination, and became the first skater to land a quadruple/double jump combination in competition.

Six years later, at the 1997 Champions Series final in Hamilton, Elvis nailed a quadruple toe/triple toe jump combination, becoming the first skater to land a quadruple/triple jump combination in competition and winning the gold medal. A month later, he repeated the feat at Worlds in Lausanne, Switzerland. Again, he won gold.

For Elvis, the years between these historic events were a steady progression up the ladder of competitive figure skating. There were high points and low points along the way, but one element was constant: his drive to achieve his personal best – always pushing himself, both mentally and physically, to the limits.

Also, with the passing years came experience and maturity. Elvis developed a formidable presence, captivating his public from the moment he stepped onto the ice.

Elvis' artistry has always reflected his great qualities: his courage, his strength, his sense of honour, and his sensitivity. His moves are precise and refined. One look, one step, and a new world of emotions is defined - a world so intense and so real, that spectators are no longer in their seats, they are out there with Elvis, sharing his experience, breathing the same breath and living the same dream.

As a result of his unique personality, and of his desire to be distinct, and to be true to himself and to his beliefs, Elvis has developed an utterly new and unique style. On the ice, he is the noble warrior fighting and reaching for a better performance. He delivers not just incredible technical feats but also magnificent artistry.

All this is truly extraordinary, but it did not happen overnight, Elvis worked very hard; he never gave up and, every year, he steadily improved.

Elvis burst onto the national scene in 1990 when, at the age of 17, he placed second (to Kurt Browning) at the Canadian Championships. He participated in his first World Championships in March that year at the Metro Centre in Halifax and later, in the Fall, he won the Trophée de France.

Skating in Munich at the World Championships in March of 1991 was a tremendous experience. The competition took place at the site of the 1972 Summer Olympic Games, in the "Olympia Halle," which had been the venue for the gymnastics event.

The site was impressive, and Elvis entered the record book by becoming the first skater to land a quad combination in competition.

It is fair to say that, at this time, Elvis started to clearly show his potential on the international scene, starting a steady climb up the standings at Worlds, improving, not just on a technical level, but artistically as well.

In Munich, Elvis was ranked sixth. He was well on his way to move into medal contention level.

The 1991-92 season was a big year for Elvis. In October 1991, he won gold at Skate Canada in London. The Canadian Championships were held in Moncton in January 1992. Elvis had a stress fracture in his left foot, but was determined to skate. He placed second, winning silver.

Elvis' foot was still bothering him a month later when the Olympic Games were held in Albertville, France. Nevertheless, he skated what he felt to be two of his best performances ever. However, although he was the only competitor to skate both a clean short program and a clean long program, he managed only a seventh place finish.

At the 1992 Worlds, held a month later in Oakland, California, Elvis won the bronze. At last, he was recognized as a major force in the world of figure skating.

San Francisco

In November 1992, Elvis won gold at Skate Canada in Victoria. The victory – his second consecutive one at this international competition – was seen as another turning point.

The Skate Canada win was followed by a second place finish in the NHK Trophy competition in Tokyo in December 1992.

Hamilton hosted the Canadian Championships in February 1993. Elvis won the silver medal.

At the Worlds, held in Prague, Czechoslovakia the following month, a disappointed Elvis was in fifth place after his short program. However, he skated an extraordinary long program (including eight clean triples), and he won silver.

Prague

1994 was the break-through year. It seemed that the door at which Elvis had been knocking for so long finally opened to him.

Canadians were held in Edmonton in January. Elvis won the short program decisively. Then, in the long program, Elvis completed eight triples. He skated with passion and, finally, he received artistic marks that were high enough to carry him over the top. He had won his first Canadian Championships gold medal.

The 1994 Olympic Games were held in Lillehammer, Norway. Elvis felt a new confidence in the fact that he was going to the Olympics as Canada's newly-crowned men's champion. He was also very happy with his programs: a techno-hip-hop short program, and a long program skated to the soundtrack of *Dragon: The Bruce Lee Story*, a movie about his martial arts idol. Elvis skated magnificently but, in a very close decision, the judges awarded him the silver and Alexei Urmanov of Russia won the gold. This silver medal had a special meaning in view of the fact that two returning champions and former Olympic gold medalists, Brian Boitano and Victor Petrenko, did not make it to the podium.

A month after the Olympic Games, Elvis was vindicated at the World Championships in Chiba, Japan. In his long program, he tried a quadruple toe/triple toe combination jump, which would have been the first such jump ever landed in competition. Unfortunately, he stepped out of the triple jump. But, he was happy that he had at least tried the jump: "It's not a matter of a skater going for perfection, which can't be achieved. It's a matter of a skater going for excellence, which can be achieved."

Elvis was given one 6.0 in technical marks (from the American judge) for his long program, along with eight 5.9s. He received four 5.9s in artistic marks, as well as four 5.8s and one 5.7. All nine judges ultimately placed him on top and Elvis finished a spectacular season by winning his first world title. Philippe Candeloro (of France) placed second, and Viacheslav Zagorodniuk (of Ukraine) was third.

The 1994-95 season started out positively. Elvis won both Skate Canada and the Nations Cup, and headed to the Canadian Championships in Halifax in January. However, Elvis' hopes of winning Canadians ended when, during a practice session, he slid into the boards and tore the anterior ligament of his right ankle. In spite of the injury, Elvis was determined to skate his short program. He wanted to defend the title that represented so many years of work, so many hopes and dreams. Reluctant to simply "hand the title over to someone else," he insisted on giving it his "best shot." However, the pain was too great, and he was forced to withdraw partway through the program. He refocused, and for the next seven weeks, fighting constant pain, he prepared himself for Worlds. He would not give up. Although he could not land a triple jump until just two weeks before leaving for the competition, he fought his way back – a result of not only of his own unwavering determination, but also of his superb physical condition prior to the fall.

The World Championships in Birmingham, England in March 1995 will always be regarded as one of the greatest highlights of Elvis Stojko's career. Having finished second to Todd Eldredge (of the United States) in the short program, Elvis opened his long program by nailing a triple Axel/triple toe combination.

However, the most spectacular moment was left for the end, when Elvis upgraded a planned triple Lutz/double toe combination jump to a triple/triple. The result? The judges, in a 6-3 split, gave Elvis the gold medal. (The French judge even awarded him a perfect 6.0 for technical merit.) Todd Eldredge won the silver medal, and Philippe Candeloro the bronze.

The I.S.U. Champions Series was inaugurated in the 1995-96 season. Skating associations from five countries – Canada, the United States, France, Germany and Japan – formed a business consortium, with revenue derived mainly from the sale of television rights, the sale of advertising space on rink boards, and from title sponsorship. Each year, skaters would be assigned two of the following five international events as a means of winning points: Skate Canada, Skate America, Trophée de France (later renamed Trophée Lalique), Nations Cup and the NHK Trophy. Substantial prize money was involved. Skaters could participate in more than their two events, but they could win only money in additional competitions, not points. When the five events finished each season, the top six men and women, and the top four in pairs and ice dancing would advance to the final.

Elvis' two assigned events in the first year of the Champions Series were Trophée de France and NHK. He placed first in both. The Champions Series final was held in Paris, in February 1996. Elvis landed a quad toe loop during his long program and he won the silver medal.

Champions Series final - Paris

Champions Series final - Paris, Palais Omnisports

Elvis regained his Canadian title in Ottawa in January 1996.

The World Championships were held in Edmonton in March 1996. For Elvis, it was a bittersweet competition. In the short program, he lost an edge and fell on a triple Axel/triple toe jump, but his long program was a triumph – a benchmark performance in the history of figure skating. He completed a quadruple/double toe combination, a triple Axel/triple toe combination (the one he had missed in the short program), a triple Axel, and a triple Lutz/double toe combination. The roar of the crowd grew with each jump, and Elvis was given a standing ovation. He later described his long program as simply: "the greatest skate of my life."

Todd Eldredge won the gold medal; Ilia Kulik (of Russia) won the silver medal; and Rudy Galindo (of the United States) won bronze. Elvis placed fourth.

1996 Worlds, Edmonton

1996 Worlds, Edmonton

Elvis clearly dominated the men's scene at the Canadian Championships in Vancouver in February 1997. He skated a powerful long program (to the soundtrack from the movie *Dragonheart*), landing a solid quadruple toe/double toe combination jump. In all, he completed six triple jumps, two in combination with double toes. And, he brought down the house at the end of the program with four spectacular flying camel jumps and an excellent spin sequence.

Elvis easily won his third Canadian men's title. He then turned his attention to the Champions Series final.

Skate Canada and NHK were the two Champions Series events assigned to Elvis in the 1996-97 season. He won both, and advanced to the final in Hamilton, in March 1997. There, he made figure skating history.

In his long program at the Champions Series final, Elvis became the first skater to complete a quadruple/triple jump combination in competition. He nailed seven triples, and was awarded his third 6.0 (in technical marks) in international competition. If he had not fallen out of a triple Axel, it is quite possible that he would have received all perfect 6.0s in technical marks from the seven-judge panel.

Elvis won the gold medal in Hamilton; Todd Eldredge won the silver medal; and Alexei Urmanov won the bronze.

The 1997 World Championships were held in Lausanne, Switzerland. Elvis' goal was quite straightforward: to regain the world title that he had lost in Edmonton the previous year.

Elvis skated his short program in Lausanne perfectly – yet he placed only fourth. Alexei Urmanov was first. Doug Leigh later explained: "We got caught in the crossfire of great skating."

Elvis' long program was the most technically loaded program ever attempted at Worlds, and he missed nothing. He did a triple flip; repeated the history-making quadruple toe/triple toe combination; completed a triple toe loop; then a triple Axel/triple toe at the halfway mark; another triple Axel; then a triple Salchow; and, finally, a triple Lutz/double toe. He received one 6.0 technical mark (from the Italian judge), and the rest were 5.9s.

Todd Eldredge knew that he needed all eight triples in his program; he couldn't afford one mistake. However, he popped a triple.

Elvis won his third world title with first place standings from eight of the nine judges. (The American judge placed Todd Eldredge first.) Eldredge ended up in second place, followed by Alexei Yagudin (of Russia).

In these words, Elvis summed up the importance of the Lausanne victory: "To be able to come back after last year, and push away everything, and still believe in myself, that's what makes it special."

What lies ahead for Elvis Stojko? He has made no secret of his goal to achieve his personal best by winning the gold medal at the 1998 Olympic Games in Nagano, Japan. But, beyond that, the future is not clear. At Skate Canada in Kitchener, in November 1996, the subject of the 2002 Olympic Games (to be held in Salt Lake City, Utah) came up in conversation. Elvis responded: "1998 is the plan, but it could extend. You never know. I always keep it open-ended. If things are going well and I feel like I can give more, it's possible. Nothing's written in stone."

Elvis as Elvis

Ever since I was a kid, rock music has been an important part of my life. So many different songs have affected me in so many different ways. Their energy, their electricity, and their intensity have inspired my skating. Even when I wasn't training, I played rock music.

My parents were always big fans of Elvis Presley and, for years, people asked me when I was going to do an Elvis number. In 1994, I finally put something together. But I waited for just the right time to introduce it. When I won the Canadian title that year, I brought out the Elvis program.

I really had fun with the Elvis routine because I love rock music — but that's not the only kind of music that inspires me. I like classical music; I like new age and techno; ambiance and alternative are great, too.

Any good music has the power to inspire and motivate me. I don't choose certain music in order to be different or to attain a unique style. I choose it because it *is* me, and because I have always been true to myself.

Over the years, a person grows and changes, maturing and understanding more as time passes. I've always listened carefully to advice, but I have always made my own decisions. What I do as a skater really comes from my heart. It's not fake. It's not done because someone told me it would impress judges — or, for that matter, anyone else.

I've always been an individual. I have always believed in doing the right thing for the right reason, and for myself. And this has had a major influence on my choice of music. I look for music that I will enjoy, and that will inspire me to skate my best. I figure that if I'm happy out there, enjoying myself and skating to great music, the people watching me will have fun, too.

When I first performed the Elvis number at Canadians in Edmonton in 1994, it was a real hit. I had put together a medley of two of my favourite Elvis hits: "Fools Rush In" and "Jailhouse Rock." It was great music for skating and, most importantly, it was music that everyone knew and could identify with.

Before I started working on the program, I watched a few tapes of Elvis. I wanted to incorporate his style into the final routine — not to copy him, but just to give hints here and there of how he moved, especially in terms of his hips and legs.

I studied the really unique way he projected his personality on stage. There was no one else like him! But, it was important to me to bring out my own personality in the program, too.

I enjoyed the routine, and the reaction to it was great. Since then, I have performed it on tours, and when I won my first World Championship. And people went wild when I skated my tribute to "The King" in Memphis a few years ago!

I'm sure that I'll continue to do Elvis Presley programs, but probably not as often as some people might like. The last thing I want is to hear people saying, "Oh, no, Elvis is doing Elvis — again." I think I should save Elvis for special occasions.

Each program that I put together is done for a reason. It has to be special, not done just for the sake of doing it. I always want to do something respectable — something that I can be proud of, and that people will relate to and enjoy.

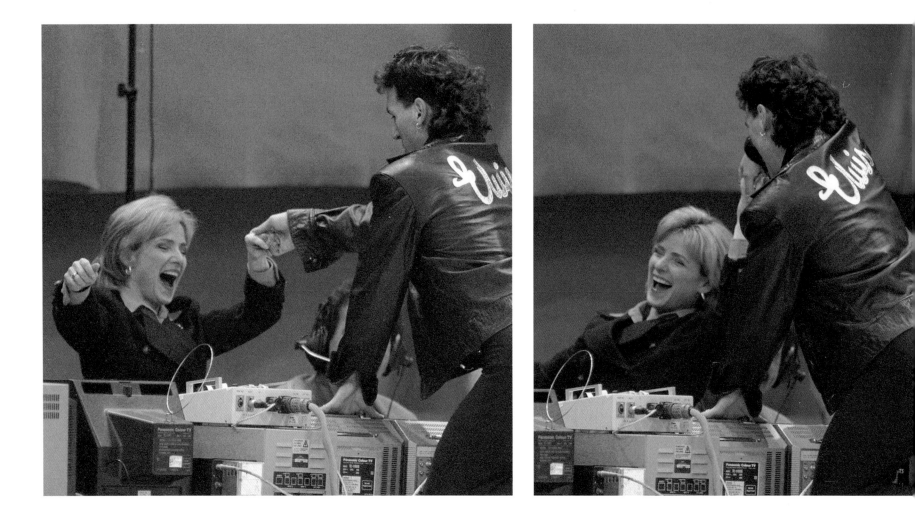

The reaction of the public has always been important to me. When people like what I'm doing, it inspires me to try that much harder. I love connecting with the audience. It gives me a feel for what they like and what they don't like, and helps me come up with new ideas.

The music has to be familiar, but yet different — something they haven't heard before in terms of skating. I've gotten a lot of reaction from using very different kinds of music — even heavy metal rock.

People say, "Hey, you know, we really like what you did. We liked the music you picked because it's different." If it's something that people like to listen to on the radio, they just love it when they hear it on the ice. Often, they ask me where the music came from, and if they can find it on tape or CD. They want to know who wrote it, who sang it.

Music really draws people together. It is a universal language. People react to music, movement, body language. You don't have to say a word. I think that's the biggest kick I get out of performing — the response of people. The music and my movements on the ice convey the excitement and the joy of figure skating to them. I think that's why I love it so much.

Creating and Innovating

ombining skating and music is like creating a whole new world. It lets me become a different person, with different feelings — expressing deep emotions through the music and my movements on the ice. For me, it can be a real escape — gliding, holding an edge, feeling the wind blow in my face. I feel free!

Since 1992, I have been working with Uschi Keszler — an inspiration as my choreographer and friend. She has always believed in the importance of what is *within* the artist. The best way of explaining what I mean by this is to compare it to a painter being given the tools to create a work of art. First, the painter is taught the technique of painting a picture: the technical aspects of how to draw, the mixing of colours, the brush strokes. Once all these things are mastered, the artist feels confident enough to begin to express himself freely — not bound by "the rules." Uschi has taught me the "brush strokes" — how to paint colours on the ice and how to be dynamic in certain ways, speeding up or slowing down — creating illusions to draw an audience in. At the same time, she has worked with me on maintaining my focus. I am able to concentrate, while still being aware of the audience. I can project to them but, at the same time, focus on what I have to do.

I am my own person. I have never believed in having someone tell me what I should do in order to "look good." An artist must be true to himself. What I do comes from within, from what I feel, from what I believe. This has been the approach that Uschi and I have taken since Day One.

A lot of people think that Uschi puts my programs together. Actually, I think it is more accurate to say that she has given me the brush strokes I was talking about. She helps me organize things but, in the end, all the movements, all the expressions, and all of the program are mine. She has never told me to do anything in a certain way. Every movement in every program comes from my own mind, my own heart, my own soul.

It takes time to mature, to develop — and it takes a very long time to understand who you are as an individual, and how to express yourself effectively. It's like learning a new language. It takes a while before people can fully understand what you're trying to say!

It's the same thing with movement. Stringing new movements together in a program, trying to express yourself to others, is sort of like stringing new words

together in sentences and trying to convey what you feel. It can be really frustrating if you don't succeed.

Over the last few years, I have reached the point where I believe that I now really *can* express myself freely. I know who I am, where I'm going, what I want.

It hasn't happened overnight, and it hasn't been easy. But, I have always believed that the shortest, easiest route isn't always the best. Taking more time, working harder — it pays off in the end.

I have watched many different skaters over the years, and I have learned a lot from them. I have trained hard in order to reach my goals.

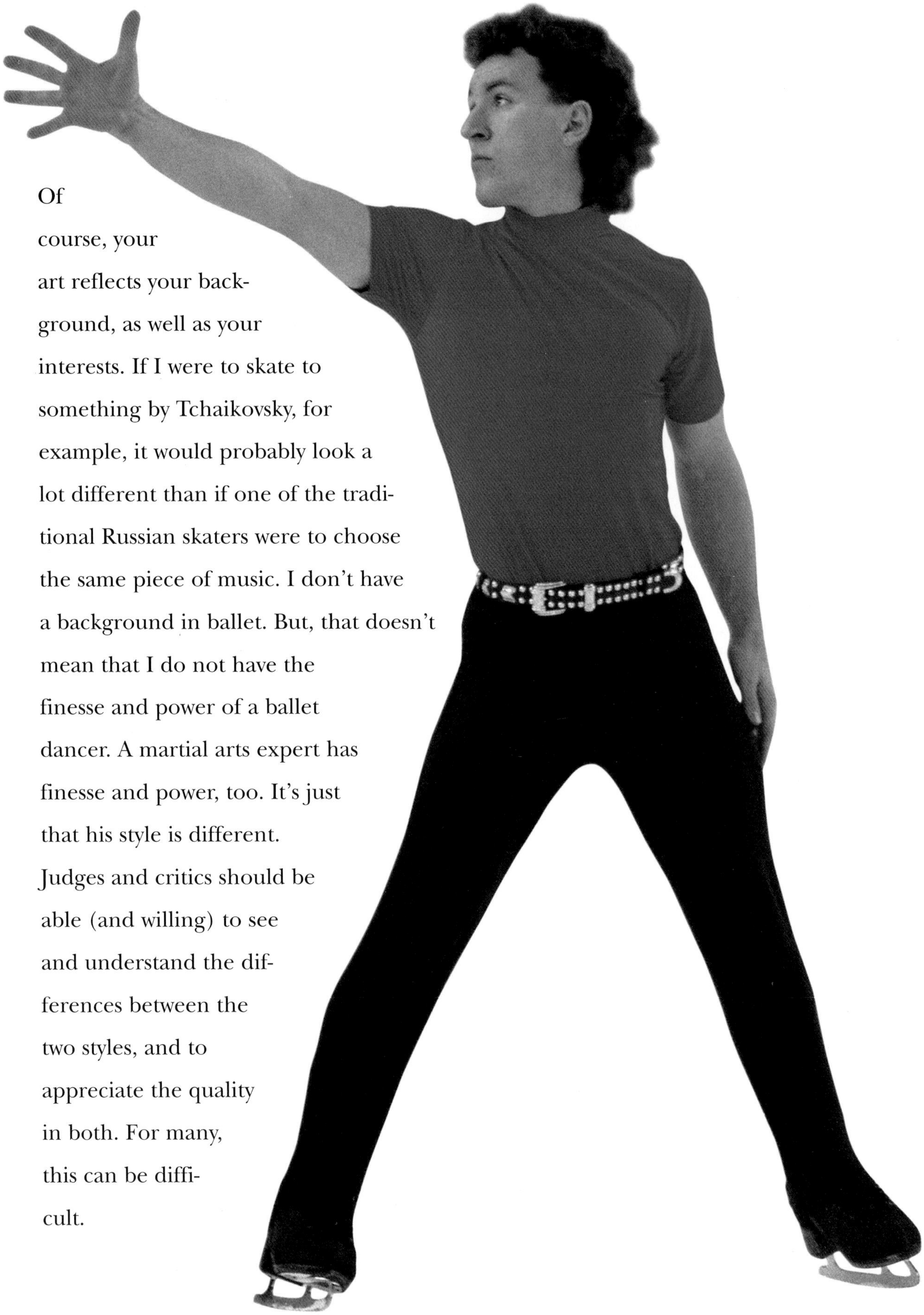

Of

course, your

art reflects your back-

ground, as well as your

interests. If I were to skate to

something by Tchaikovsky, for

example, it would probably look a

lot different than if one of the tradi-

tional Russian skaters were to choose

the same piece of music. I don't have

a background in ballet. But, that doesn't

mean that I do not have the

finesse and power of a ballet

dancer. A martial arts expert has

finesse and power, too. It's just

that his style is different.

Judges and critics should be

able (and willing) to see

and understand the dif-

ferences between the

two styles, and to

appreciate the quality

in both. For many,

this can be diffi-

cult.

I know that I have everything it takes to go where I want to go. I've just got to keep on striving — believing in those brush strokes made by the blades of my skates, the dynamics created on the ice by my choice of music and movements, the feelings that I convey to the audience.

The learning process never ends. But, considering my accomplishments to date, it is fair to say that I now see myself as the artist that Uschi and I envisioned years ago. There are people whose vision may be too narrow to recognize this, but I won't let them stand in my way. I must remain focused, keep pushing, do the best that I can, and achieve my goals.

Practice

Makes Perfect

"To strive, to seek, to find, and not to yield."
Tennyson, *Ulysses* (1842)

I love going to the rink, whether it's six o'clock in the morning, one o'clock in the afternoon, or seven o'clock at night. I'm happy sweating it out and pushing myself to my limits every day. Through practice, I expand those limits; my understanding of skating grows; I learn how to cope in pressure situations.

Practice cannot make you *perfect*. That would be an impossible goal. But it can result in a performance that is *excellent*. I have always strived for excellence.

Many skaters go to competitions unprepared. They want to win, but aren't willing to devote the necessary time to training. You can have all the talent in the world, but if you are not properly prepared, you will never be able to achieve your goals. I have always pushed myself on practice.

It is very important to stay focused in practice. I treat my hours of training very seriously, very much like an actual competition. Some people wonder why I am so serious about practice. They do not understand that my strength as a skater, as an artist, grows as a result of the consistency of practice — pushing myself to the limits (and beyond!) every day, working hard and concentrating on my goals. The physical and mental effort can be exhausting but, in the end, it's worth it. It's great to have a gold medal hanging around your neck!

I've never believed in giving up. The extra effort is worth it. I always push forward. It doesn't mean that I'll be perfect. I make mistakes — but I learn from my mistakes, and move on. Judges and critics like to talk about "artistry." Artistry starts with technique. To have technique, to have great power, you have to have what is called "edge quality." To build speed and power, you have to have a great base — and that base always starts from the blades up, with the edges. Years ago, when I started working with Uschi, she told me that I had good edge quality and that we could build on it to achieve speed, and strength, and finesse. When compulsory figures were removed from competition, we took the time that had been spent on them and, instead, spent hour after hour working on simple edges and footwork in my free skating, developing my skills.

Uschi's many years of research have helped improve the quality of my edges. This has given me a great feel for artistic impression, where most or all of the movement comes from the blades up — from the legs and the edges, and the connection between them. If you don't have that connection, you lose balance; your edges don't flow as well as they should; you make too much noise. When a good skater goes by, you will rarely hear the edge. There is not a lot of friction, so the skater can go faster. That's where the speed comes from!

When I trained for a while with Shae-Lynn Bourne and Victor Kraatz, they worked on edges a lot, too — along with all the technical stuff that took up our time. It was a great opportunity for me. We came up with some super ideas and exercises that were a lot of fun. They are hard to explain on paper but, basically, had to do with just regular basic turns, rockers, counters, brackets — in series and in circles — and also doing movements through those edges and turns that allowed us to work on balance. We worked on the right foot, then the left foot, and then the switching up of feet. We worked on turns — quick turns between going fast and going slow, then accelerating and decelerating at a very quick pace — and learning control.

Control is basically the result of body position and balance — and balance, as I said before, is based on edge quality. If you can develop good edge quality, you will have more control. If you are using less effort to balance yourself, then you can do more movements.

A key factor with many skaters is maintaining balance. If you watch them, they move from one side to another, but they are not actually doing any movements. They are just trying to balance themselves.

A skilled skater will often use off-balance control in order to show movement. You can tell the difference between one skater who is trying to balance himself and another who deliberately puts himself off-balance to get a movement across, then regains control. This can be a very good exercise!

Physical conditioning is important. Over the years, I've been involved in a lot of different sports. I've never done weights, but my body structure is good — and I've spent a lot of time on martial arts. But, most of my exercise is on the ice. As my strength has increased through practice, my jumps have gotten bigger and more powerful.

It is important to have power — but, it is also important to have control over that power. There is no point in having a car with lots of horsepower if you can't keep it from going all over the road! It's the same thing with figure skating. If you can't control your power, you won't be very balanced, and you won't be able to do what you want to do, and do it correctly. You must be very exact, very controlled — able to take that power and focus it in one spot.

You can have raw power but without control, it is useless. In martial arts, I have often used focus and explosion training to help me learn more about my body, the power that I have, and how to control that power. Experimenting with martial arts has been fun. I've enjoyed it as something quite apart from skating — but it's also great relating back and forth between the two sports, and bringing elements of one to the other.

There are similarities in movement between martial arts and skating. For example, in martial arts, you explode, and that is where you get the power to deliver a punch. In skating, you use your finesse to explode into a jump. But, probably the most important thing that I've learned through martial arts is how to increase my ability to focus. This has had a major impact on my skating. I can focus on a particular part of my body and be able to correct something that I'm not doing properly. I am aware of each different aspect of a technique.

Elvis during a Kung Fu practice with his instructor and friend Glen Doyle

73

When it comes to jumping, it is necessary to focus on more than just one aspect of technique. At this level, I have to concentrate on the whole package. One slight mistake — like over-rotating a bit on the take-off, can throw me off a jump. If the jump does not go up square in the air, with hips and shoulders square to the take-off, it just won't work. I now know my jumps inside and out, and if I am doing something wrong, I can correct it, put the jump back together again, and then go out and do it — properly. This is the key to competition. You have to understand how a jump works, so that you can fix it when it needs fixing. That's where confidence enters the picture, and that's when you know you're ready for competition.

I go over the jump again and again until I achieve the quality that is my goal, until the jump feels "right." I know that if I can do this in practice, I can do it in competition, too. And, that is what I strive for.

In the martial arts, there is time for practice and time for relaxation. This has been a great help to me in terms of focusing. When you are relaxed, you can focus a lot more easily than when you are hyper and over-energetic. It's important to be "up" for a competition, but you shouldn't be too up; you shouldn't be too hyper; and you shouldn't have too much energy, because you might not be able to control it. In competition, it is important to be able to bring the power and energy you are feeling down to a level that you can control. This comes with practice and experience. It is where young skaters often run into problems, and they don't understand what has gone wrong. They prepare a program and feel ready for competition. But the program doesn't go well. After they leave the ice, they feel that, given the chance, they could go back out and now give the performance of a lifetime. The reason? It's because they have burned off all that excess energy that they didn't need.

You have to be able to focus, to control your energy. You need to make it your ally, instead of trying to harness it, to muscle it. That wastes your energy, too. There has to be a harmony between you and your body. Your mind, and your body, and your soul have to connect in order to move forward. And this comes through relaxation.

Coaches are an important factor when it comes to competition. Often, I can be alone at practice in competition, because I know myself so well. But the input of a coach can be really helpful if you are having a problem, or if he or she sees something that is slightly "off," but you can't figure out exactly what is wrong. What you cannot feel, a coach may be able to see. The moral support of a coach is also really important. By the time you get to competition, there will not be a lot of input from a coach. The groundwork has been laid. There is just fine tuning here and there, small adjustments — nothing major. But it's great to know that there is someone there if something goes wrong, someone to talk to, someone to provide feedback.

The last words of advice I usually get at competition are:"Go out there. You can do it for yourself". And, I just look at Doug and Uschi, and answer: "Okay, I know I can do it. See you back here in four and a half minutes!"

Building a program starts in April or May, and goes on throughout the year. There are specific times when I work with Uschi - a week here and a week there - just on the program itself, not the technical stuff. We put it all together later.

A lot of times, I work by myself. I may concentrate on jumps until I get a bit tired, then go back and do parts of my program, structuring and fine-tuning it.

A lot of the movements are the result of constant improvisation. We put on some music and I do whatever comes out naturally on the ice. Uschi and I will develop some ideas, and she'll watch me try them out. I know we're making progress when I hear her say: "This looks great! This looks great! This looks great!" Then we start putting the pieces together.

A lot of ideas come from just messing around and having a good time on the ice — putting on the music and just going free with it. The movements come out naturally, and are great to play with. I can combine them with the technical aspects and come up with a really super program — one that works for me, and one in which the movements are mine.

I don't treat choreography as something quite separate from regular practice. I try to intertwine the two. It's true that sometimes I spend my time working just on jumps and spins, but often I join them together and play with ideas involving those jumps and spins. This results in the creation of movements that I then put into the program.

I also go through the program and separate out the movements that need more of my time. I concentrate on them until I feel they are just right. It is important that the movements feel good when I'm going into a jump, and when I'm coming out of a jump; when I'm going into a spin, and when I'm coming out of a spin. You have to feel comfortable going into that quad combination. You don't want a movement to throw you off; you want your centre of gravity to be very stable before you attempt something so technically difficult.

Putting together a program doesn't happen overnight. When June rolls around, Uschi and I may still be working on some new ideas and trying to fit them in with what we've already got.

Practice or competition, Elvis can count on practical video assistance from his mom.

It's not always easy to find the time, especially with my touring schedule. Also, you've got to be in the right frame of mind. A painter can't just sit down in front of a canvas and create a work of art. He has to be in the right mood; he has to be in a "creative mode." That's when the artistic juices flow!

The
HUNTER

The hunter seeks. Relentlessly he pursues - ever further, ever faster, ever stronger. Nothing will stop him. He has no fear; he knows no pain, he will not rest. His goal? Not a kill but victory - the conquest of himself, the accomplishment of his dreams, and, for a moment, to touch perfection.

1996

was an up and
down kind of a
year. Physically, I was fine. But, emotionally, I was going through what was sometimes a very difficult
maturing process — trying to learn about and understand myself, both as a person and as a skater.

I had placed fourth at Worlds — after winning the title in '94 and '95 — and everyone seemed to be saying that, as a result, my season was a disaster. And, this was all because I fell on one jump in Edmonton!

I have to laugh at the thought that one jump could determine the success or failure of my entire year. It just isn't true. Admittedly, the jump was important. Missing it took me out of the race. But, that doesn't mean that my year was a write-off. I learned so much more from that year than from any other year I can remember. You always learn from your mistakes.

I have always been "The Hunter" — always striving, always gaining. Every day, I want to do better than I did the day before. In every competition, I want to improve upon my last skate. I always push my limits, mentally and physically. It's not simply striving for a gold medal that makes me "hunt" this way; it has been my constant drive to better myself — pushing the jumps, pushing the spins, pushing the artistry.

I have pushed everything to the limit, striving for that ultimate performance in competition, whether it be at Worlds, or at the Olympic Games. That has always been my goal. Even if you don't win, knowing that you have produced your very best possible performance is just about the best feeling that can be imagined.

The *Dragonheart* long program that I developed in the 1996-97 season was very aggressive, very attack-oriented. I have always liked "attacking" a program, and I wanted to deal with the aspect of technical difficulty in the program by: opening with a triple flip; then completing the quad/triple; moving into a triple loop; then doing the triple Axel/triple toe; next, a triple Axel and triple Salchow; and, finally, a triple Axel/triple toe.

The movie *Dragonheart* has always inspired me. It portrays dragons as the protectors of all mankind, and the perfect examples of dignity, morality, honour, truth, and pride. These are qualities that are important to me, and the program gives me a chance to express this. The slow section of the choreography enables me to show the soft side — the honour, and the dignity — that can be present in even a warrior, that indeed must be present in that warrior. I think that athletes are, in fact, warriors in their own way: reaching for that goal; striving and competing; always being in an attack mode.

The "warrior attitude" has gotten me through a lot of difficult times.

The 1996-1997 season kicked off with Skate Canada, where I knew that people were anxiously waiting to see my long program, and were worried about how I would do after what the media considered had been a terrible year. I pushed forward and won Skate Canada.

Then, when I headed for the Trophée Lalique in France, I became sick and couldn't skate. This proved be yet another test for me.

I came home, trained hard, and went to NHK in Japan, which I won. Remaining very focused, I headed for Canadians. Putting down the quad combination, I once again placed first. The next event on my schedule was the Champions Series Final in Hamilton. Here, I made history by completing the first quad/triple combination in competition! What an incredible feeling it was to then move on, repeat the quad/triple at Worlds, and win the title. I had come back from a difficult year, and accomplished what many people had believed would be impossible.

Deep down inside, I knew that I could do it; I knew I had it in me. I thought of myself as almost having the heart of a dragon — having the strength, the honour, and the dignity to go out and do it for myself. A lot of people might laugh at this, and label it a fairytale. But I believe in it. I believe in honour. People may laugh at the concept, but I know that it works.

Over the years, I have won many competitions. They may not always have involved gold

medals, but the important thing is that I have consistently achieved what I set out to do. You have to have inner strength; you must be able to realize that you are the only person who can really understand exactly what is going on in your heart, in your soul. And, that is what counts because, when you go out on that ice, you are all alone.

In 1997, everything really came together for me. Now, I am focusing on the upcoming Olympics, and hoping my dream will come true. In spite of the victories of the past season, I remain "The Hunter," in search of the ultimate performance, pushing forward to 1998.

Show
Spectacular

As well as doing my own tour and the Tom Collins tour, I do television specials. Last year's Elvis Incognito was about a year and a half in the making.

There were a lot of script changes, and we spent almost a month taping. There were long hours spent with the crew and cast members. "Hurry up!" "Get on the ice!" "Wait, something's wrong with the camera!" Sometimes, we would get backed up three, four, five, or even six hours.

It takes a lot of patience and a lot of time to create something worthwhile.

Team work is an important aspect of doing a television special. You want to be able to work well with everybody, because you will be spending a lot of time with them. The key for me has always been cooperation — and having fun making people happy!

It takes a while to put together a television special because you want it to be just right. Often, by the time taping begins, the writing and structure of the show will have changed. It's not exactly what you had in mind at the beginning. It's a lot better!

Taping of *Elvis Incognito*, "Caruso".

A television show starts with a concept and it grows from there. It changes; it is a metamorphosis. Everybody gets involved: the producer, the director, the choreographers, the coaches, the writers, and me. We all get together and basically play with ideas until we come up with what we want: what will look good on television, and what will be understood and enjoyed by the audience. It's a lot of work but, in the end, it's worth it.

Taping of *Elvis Incognito* - fight scene rehearsal.

I enjoy the weeks I spend with friends and other skaters on tour. It's important that everyone gets along; that everyone supports each other; that everyone is having a good time. The last thing I want is for skaters to be in a competitive mode on tour, stressed out if a performance doesn't go well. I believe that the idea should be to have fun — to really enjoy yourself doing something that is the result of your accomplishments in competition during the season. People are acknowledging you for who you are, and for what you have done. That's what counts in doing tours.

Show life can be fun. I've had a super time on tours: skating in shows, working with lots of different people, appearing both on and off camera. It's great. But, it can also be really tough living out of a suitcase, travelling by bus or plane, getting up early, and going to bed late.

There are hours of rehearsal required, particularly at the beginning of a tour. The amount of time involved depends upon the particular tour. For example, there are more rehearsals on the Elvis tour than on the Tom Collins tour. On the other hand, the Collins tour is a lot longer than the Elvis tour, and that makes a difference.
It's difficult to squeeze out hours for training when you're on tour. You have to structure your time carefully, and pay close attention to both your physical and mental state.

There is a great difference between the world of shows and the world of competition. Competition is very structured, and it takes a lot out of you. There is more intensity, more pressure. This is not to say that there isn't pressure involved in doing shows. When you're on tour, you want to skate well, to be in top form. But, competition requires even more than that. You have to be more focused. And youv'e got to skate even better.

Great friends: Lu Chen (above), and Michelle Kwan (right).

Show skating is a good break from competition. I enjoy being out on the ice, skating not for judges and marks, but to entertain people. It's great to be having a good time with the audience. I have been asked if there is such a thing as "instant creation." When you are out on the ice, new movements will sometimes appear, especially in show skating. Often, you are so structured in what you're doing during the competitive season, that you can't make adjustments in a program in a given situation. But, in show skating, a movement will often just come out. I enjoy that. It's a blast for me to have my body do what feels *natural* for it to do — not what has been imposed upon it.

I have a lot of feel for movement. I keep trying different things and, as a result, a program will get better and better as the year progresses. This approach works with show programs, too. When a movement comes out, and the crowd likes it, and I'm having a great time, I decide to keep that movement in the program.

Television shows are very structured — like competition — but you do have a lot of leeway. If something doesn't seem to be working, you can tape it one way and then another — maybe even three ways. Then you can pick the variation you like best, and proceed from there.

Small changes that have no effect on the structure of the show can be done on impulse. Things never work out exactly as planned. You've got to be able to roll with the punches, to go with the flow, to make changes when you can.

I think that a very key element in becoming a good skater is being able to make necessary changes when you can. Even when you have tried your best, sometimes that extra "little bit" will make it even better, make it special.

Listen to the inner voice that allows you to be you! A lot of great movements comes from pressure situations where an extra head movement, or nuance, or change is inserted that comes from the heart and soul.

There is a lot of energy involved in touring. It's really the travelling, rather than the skating, that throws you off — changes in terms of time zones, different hours getting up and going to bed. The schedule constantly changes. It's hard to rebuild your stamina when you're spending long hours on buses and planes, going to bed at 4:00 in the morning, getting up at 9:00, going to another arena to do another show.

Touring takes a toll on the body. You can't always perform exactly as you'd like, because it is impossible to maintain the peak level you have achieved during the competitive season. You have to allow yourself some "down time," some time to just enjoy the moment when you can.

Travelling is a tough road, but you make it the best you can. Training hard before starting out, and being in good physical shape, enable me to handle the schedule even when I'm tired. A lot has to do with your state of mind — what you believe in, and what you think you can do under the circumstances. You can't push yourself too hard, because you don't want to risk injury. You've got to know the limitations of your body. That comes with time, and with experience.

There are many positive aspects in terms of touring: getting to really know yourself, as well as other skaters; discovering what audiences like, and what they don't like; developing your skills in terms of connecting with an audience; trying out new ideas that can be used down the line in competition programs; and finding out just how far you can push yourself. All are invaluable if you plan to continue on the show circuit as well as the competition circuit.

Spirit to Compete

"The important thing in life is not the victory but the contest; the essential thing is not to have won, but to have fought well."

Baron Pierre de Coubertin (1908)

I believe that the driving force behind me as a competitor is the pursuit of excellence.

Every day, I try to improve myself, as an athlete and as a person. I get to know myself better when I compete — how I react to competition, how I interact with other competitors. I have learned that although you can't always control the outcome in a particular situation, the way you deal with it can make it easier the next time around. I have made this philosophy a part of my everyday life, not just my skating, and I think that it has made me a better human being.

A skater goes through a lot of different feelings during competition. Staying calm is the key point. You feel a little anxious, a little nervous, a little unsettled. That's when you've got to trust your feelings, trust your abilities. Believe in what you have worked for so long to achieve. Have faith in yourself.

Often, I meditate to centre myself. In my head, I focus on the competition ahead. I picture myself doing well. I envision everything: the sensations, the feelings, the smallest detail. It takes a lot of time and effort to be able to reach this point, but it really helps me to maintain focus.

During competition, I don't do any interviews. I spend a lot of time by myself, relaxing, watching television, going for walks, listening to music. I practise a bit before I compete, then I get myself prepped. I pump myself up; I get centered; I picture the outcome only as being good. I focus on the outcome not in terms of winning, but in terms of competing well, of skating well. I have no control over anything beyond that. If I win, I win. If I don't win, I don't win.

The most important thing is control — my control of myself, and of my skating. This is what I concentrate on the most, always trying to be calm, to be centred, and to be focused. I remind myself that I'm here because I enjoy it, not because anyone is pressuring me. I tell myself to relax, to enjoy myself, to trust myself.

1994 was a great year. It always stands out as the real push forward in terms of moving into the upper echelon of figure skating competition. Winning the '94 Canadian championship was a major high for me. Then, going to Lillehammer and placing second at the end of competition was incredible.

The situation that year was an unusual one as a result of the new rules that allowed professional skaters, such as Brian Boitano and Victor Petrenko, to be reinstated as amateurs. I had been ranked fourth in overall slotting for the competition, so coming second and winning the silver medal was a really great achievement for me. And, it was amazing to win the World title in Japan after the Olympics were over.

I have now won three World titles, as well as the silver medal at the Olympics. I have won; I have lost; and I have won again. I've travelled in both directions on the road — and I've learned a lot on the way.

I injured myself during Canadians in 1995. In spite of the pressure, I managed to maintain my focus. I had been World champion the year before, but I had to think of 1995 in terms of being a clean sheet of ice. I told myself that everything happens for a reason, that you have to play the game with the cards you are dealt.

After I hit the boards in Halifax, a lot of people asked me why I even tried to skate. But, I had worked for so long to win that competition! I'd taken the title from Kurt Browning the year before and, having pushed myself so far and having accomplished so much, I didn't want to just hand the title over to someone else. I had to defend it. I knew that whatever would happen, would happen. But, deep down inside, I also knew that if I did not skate, I would always wonder, "What if . . . ?" You always regret the things you don't do; you never regret the things you do. Even if you make a mistake, it is important to know that you tried — that, at least, you gave it your best shot.

As it turned out, my best shot wasn't enough. There was, however, one very positive aspect to this difficult situation. I had worked very, very hard in the months leading up to competition and was in really good physical condition. When the doctors said that I wouldn't be able to compete at Worlds, I refused to believe them.

Training that season was tough. I didn't attempt a triple jump until two or three weeks after the accident. I couldn't do a triple Axel until a couple of days before I left for Birmingham. I did manage to work on edges — but only for brief periods of times, and not very often. I really couldn't do too much. I had to pace myself. At first, I took it minute by minute. Then I took it session by session, day by day. Eventually, I was able to get back in top form.

It was an incredible, character-building experience. Being able to come back and win in Birmingham, after what had happened in Halifax, taught me a valuable lesson. I discovered the importance of believing in myself. If you push forward, confident that you can accomplish something, you will achieve your goal.

1996 Worlds came at the end of what for me had been a difficult season. A relationship I was involved in had ended, and I was having a tough time dealing with that. There was a lot of pressure on me that year because Worlds were being held in Canada. I just wanted to concentrate on my own strategy for Edmonton, my own skating. But, it wasn't easy getting focused. Physically, I felt fine; mentally, I was being pulled in different directions.

After I fell in the short program, I almost felt a sense of relief. The pressure was gone. I had made a mistake, but I believed that it must have happened for a reason. I was convinced that the way in which I handled the situation would make a difference. I couldn't let myself get caught up in what the media were saying about me and about my skating.

It wasn't easy, but I dealt with what had happened as well as I could. I decided that I was going to skate my long program to the very best of my ability. I just had to trust in myself.

I gained a lot of confidence and understanding that year. It was a real learning experience. You may fail as often as you succeed, but you always learn from those failures. Something good comes out of every experience. The next year, I felt stronger and more positive, much more focused on exactly what I wanted out of my skating, and out of myself.

I had discovered where my strengths lay. I had found out who my real friends were, and how much those friends — and my family — meant to me. But, most importantly, I had realized that I was my own best friend, and that I needed more time to be by myself.

Winning a gold medal isn't the only thing that counts. What's important is doing your best, for yourself — whatever the circumstances may be. In 1996, I was in neutral, just idling. I wasn't able to get going; I didn't know what to focus on. Everything changed in 1997. I focused not so much on winning, but on the job at hand — feeling good about myself and about my skating. That's what produces results, and that's what wins competitions.

I won every competition that I entered in the '97 season, staying very, very focused and knowing exactly what I wanted. But I knew that even my win in Lausanne at Worlds wouldn't change the situation in terms of the Olympics in 1998. In Nagano, I would still be "The Hunter" — hunting for that ultimate performance, hunting for the excellence that has always been my goal.

Winning comes second; it should be pushed to the back of your mind. Instead, you have to concentrate on pushing forward, on making a difference both in your sport and in yourself as an individual. This is what has always been my focus — not the winning, the fame, and the money. Those things will happen, if what you do comes from the heart, and if you believe in yourself.

Believing in myself is very important to me. It is what got me through the season in '96; what enabled me to accomplish what I did in '97; and what I'm going to focus on for the Olympics in '98.

Olympic Fervour

y first Olympic Games were in Albertville, in 1992. I can still recall the thrill of walking with the other members of the team, behind the Canadian flag, into the Olympic Stadium for the opening ceremonies.

I could have left to get set up for Worlds as soon as my events were finished, but I wanted to be both in the opening and closing ceremonies. I was worried that I mightn't ever get a second chance to take part in something so amazing.

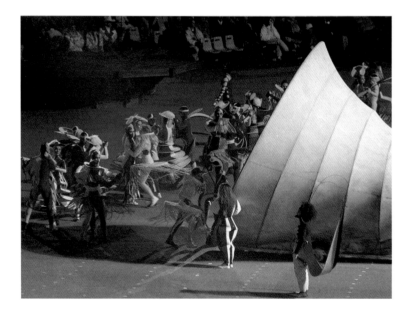

When I look back at the '92 Olympics, I think that what stands out in my memory is, simply, the skating. I had worked so long and so hard — and I skated two of my best performances ever. I was the only competitor to skate both a clean short program *and* a clean long program.

Skating at the Olympics is so different from skating at Worlds. It's not easy to explain. I guess it's that the Olympic Games are the pinnacle for which every amateur athlete strives. But thinking about the Games is one thing; actually taking part in them is another.

I still remember how it felt: doing a movement, looking down, and seeing the Olympic rings — right in the centre of the ice! I skated over them, realizing that, even though it was a little overwhelming, it was also inspirational. The dream that I had had since I was a kid had come true. Nothing could take this experience away from me. I had trained for so many years; I had achieved my goals; I was really there!

Of course, there are many skaters from many countries at the Olympic Games. There are also many other athletes, involved in many different sports. It's great to meet them, and to have the opportunity to see what they do. And, it's always fun to renew acquaintances with people you have met in previous competitions.

After I arrived at the Olympic site in 1992, I was directed to the building where I had to get my accreditation. When I walked in. I realized that I was one of the smallest people there! I was surrounded by a crowd of athletes representing a wide range of sport and countries. Some of them were huge — over 6 feet tall! It was absolute mayhem — everyone running around, getting registered, having pictures taken for accreditation.

It was a lot of fun. One of the things you realize at Olympics is that all the athletes — however famous they may be — have one important thing in common. Their sports may differ, but they have all worked hard to achieve the same goal — participating in the Games.

After the skating events had been completed, we had a chance to watch some other sports, and do some skiing. Mike Slipchuk, Doug Ladret, and Kurt and I hit the slopes, along with some of the other skaters, and really had a super time. It was great — wearing our Olympic jackets; meeting other athletes; and feeling a part of the whole, wonderful scene.

Representing Canada at the Olympics is a great honour, and I feel so very fortunate to have done it not just once, but twice — in Albertville in '92, and in Lillehammer in '94.

There was controversy in terms of my performance in Albertville. In spite of skating clean programs, I placed seventh. I did come back and win the bronze medal at Worlds a month later. But, nevertheless, the Olympics were the big accomplishment for me that year. It was there that I at last stepped "out of the shadow," and where I was finally recognized as a force in the skating world. When I returned home from the 1992 Olympics, my aunt and uncle gave me a medallion they had made especially for me. A lot of people have asked me about the medallion,

because I have worn it in every competition since then. It's round, and on it are engraved the words Sixteenth Olympic Winter Games, along with the Olympic rings. On the back, it says: Congratulations, Elvis. You're Number One. My aunt and uncle realized that I had put down a really great skate; that I had achieved my goal; and that my Olympic dream had become a reality. Their pride in my accomplishment meant a lot to me. I have been very, very lucky to have had such wonderful support from my family over the years.

With Michelle Leigh,
Dr. Peter Jensen (CFSA's
Medical/Scientific Committee) and
Doug Leigh.

Canadians show their support,
many from the *Lycée canadien de
Paris.*

Lillehammer 1994.

Lillehammer 1994.

Competition at the 1994 Olympics was unusual, as a result of the return of the professionals. I had been ranked second (to Kurt Browning) from the year before, but, with the return of Brian Boitano and Victor Petrenko, my rating changed to fourth going into the Games. I didn't really have high expectations in terms of where I would place, because I knew that I really had no control over how the other competitors would skate. I simply had to concentrate on myself, and on my own skating.

When the dust settled after the short program, I realized that I was in second place, and that Kurt was in twelfth place — and I knew that I had a shot at the gold. But I had to push that thought from my mind, and just focus on my skate.

I was happy with my long program. There was a small glitch at the beginning when I did only a single axel, but I managed to put the triple back in later. I hadn't fallen and, technically, I hadn't made a mistake. I had just singled one jump. Because I needed a packaged program, I took the quad out (rather than miss it), and put the Axel back in, with a triple toe. Everything else fell into place.

A lot of people believed that I should have placed first, that I deserved to win. But, everything happens for a reason. I think that if I had won in Lillehammer, it would have been difficult for me to build up and maintain the inspiration required for Nagano in 1998.

I have won three World titles, but I am still striving for that ultimate performance. Achieving it at the Olympic Games is my goal. If I win, I win. But, in the meantime, I simply have to concentrate on my skating — pushing myself beyond the limits, and training hard every day. That must be my focus.

For Your  Only

𝒪n March 1997, I attended the opening of
Planet Hollywood in Toronto. Before going
down to the restaurant, we dropped in at a
reception where the media was given the opportunity to interview celebrities who were taking
part in the event.

It was fun meeting and talking with stars such as
Sylvester Stallone, Demi Moore, and Bruce
Willis.

Demi and I chatted for a while about skating, and about life in Sun Valley, where she and Bruce and their
children live. It was a great experience coming face to face with people that I'd only seen on movie and television screens.

Planet Hollywood was so packed that we could barely move, but I wouldn't have missed the fun for anything! What really sticks out in my memory is the realization that celebrities are human, just like everyone else. On the screen, they seem so much larger-than-life, and almost unreal. But, they can be really down to earth, and quite "normal" when you talk with them.

I spent some time with Luke Perry. He and his wife are huge fans of figure skating; he asked me for my autograph, and I asked him for his!

Athletes were out in force at the party, too.

A lot of Toronto Raptors turned up — along with Tie Domi from the Toronto Maple Leafs. Kurt Browning was there, which was great because I hadn't seen him in a while. And, I got to chat again with Toronto Argonauts star, "Pinball" Clemens.

It was a super night, and I hated to see it end.

1997 Toronto Raptors Game - Elvis is presented to an enthusiastic crowd.

Huronia summer and winter fun.

Elvis enjoys the outdoors. He handles jet skis expertly (opposite page, near his cottage). In the winter, a fairy tale landscape is always captivating and so relaxing!

1997 Molson Indy in Toronto - Elvis is in the lead pace car and later he gives the start of the race.

Rare appearance and autograph session at a Toronto Mall.

Elvis plays a little.

The contest is close, but Elvis' dad wins most of the time.

A prized Lillehammer jacket part of Elvis' collection.

1997 Canadians (opposite page) - spectators did not, at first, notice that one of the helpers repairing the ice was Elvis, but when they did, ice resurfacing became a new center of attention! And of course a reward was soon in Elvis' hands, one more for the collection!

Elvis is *Kids Ambassador* for Ronald McDonald Children's Charities of Canada.

This non profit organization helps children with serious illnesses and disabilities - Elvis spends time with his young friends, sharing in their activities and their hopes.

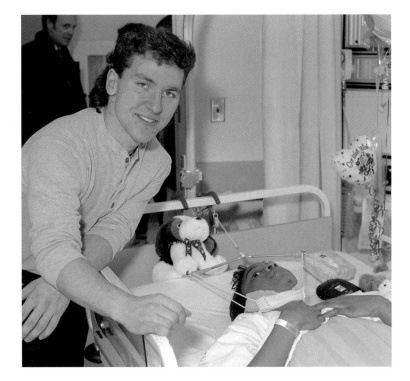

Toronto Hospital for Sick Children - Elvis meets a young gymnast recuperating from a bad fall.

164

The family home at Christmas.

Free as the Wind

there are similarities
between riding a bike and
skating. I find freedom
through both of them —
going out and "doing my
own thing," unrestricted in
any way.

About eighty-five percent of the time on my dirt bike, I'm standing up on the pegs, always jumping and adjusting to the terrain.

I love going uphill and downhill, and riding through the forest. .

I love the feel of the bike; using my body and the angles; leaning over and grabbing the right amount of pressure on the tires; coming up from the corner and going on the gas; having the power right there, right at the flick of my wrist

For me, this has always been exciting. I have spent so many hours, so many years training on the ice, using my own muscles to get from A to B. Sometimes, it's nice to have a motor beneath me, to just flick my wrist and get from A to B faster, and with a lot less exertion!

When my amateur skating days are over and I move on, I think it would be great to go on a long bike tour, either in the United States or Europe. I'd like to get away for a month or so — maybe with a couple of friends — and travel around, clear my head. Getting away from the hustle and bustle of my life as a skater would be sort of like a retreat, an escape from everything. I need that. But, right now, there just isn't time.

With a special camera on his helmet, Elvis recorded exciting footage for *Elvis Incognito.*

However, (picture below), a few rides and a technician were needed to fine tune the camera.

Riding a dirt bike is a lot different from riding a street bike. It's a little more challenging, a little more physically demanding. Dirt bikes involve aggressive driving, lots of jumps and turns, and plenty of fun, Best of all, you don't have to worry about traffic!

When I stop at the top of a hill, I shut off my motor, and just gaze — in the silence — across the countryside, I feel utterly relaxed, and my spirit is free.

178

ACKNOWLEDGEMENTS

We greatfully acknowledge the support of the following sponsors:

GENERAL MILLS CANADA, INC.

McDONALD'S RESTAURANTS OF CANADA LIMITED

CANON CANADA INC.

MASTERCARD INTERNATIONAL INCORPORATED

McCAIN FOODS LIMITED

ROOTS CANADA LTD.

Special thanks to:

Graphic Colour Imaging for production work

PHOTO CREDITS:

F. Scott Grant - *21 (upper right), 54, 85*

Michelle Harvath - *169*

Paul Harvath - *104 (all)*

Gilbert Iund, *TempSport* - *14*

Dimitri Iund, *TempSport* - *92, 147*

Masaharu Sugawara, *Japan Sports* - *16, 17 (all)*

Barb McCutcheon - *161 (upper right),162*

J-Y Ruszniewski, *TempSport* - *122*

Office of Futerman & Futerman, Stojko family - *ii, 151, 152, 153 (all), 156 (all), 165, 166*

Gérard Châtaigneau, *The Figure Skating Calendar* - *all others*

INDEX